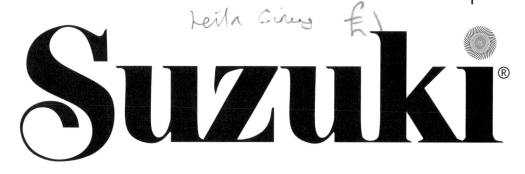

Suzuki®

CELLO SCHOOL

Volume 1
Piano Accompaniment
Revised Edition

GW00537186

ISBN 0-87487-480-7

CONTENTS

©1979 Fritz Henle

Maestro Pablo Casals

1 Twinkle, Twinkle, Little Star Variations
Variation A

S. Suzuki

Variation B

Variation C

Variation D

Theme

2 French Folk Song

Folk Song

3 Lightly Row

Folk Song

4 Song of the Wind

Folk Song

Kingston Calypso

Violoncello

Kathy & David Blackwell

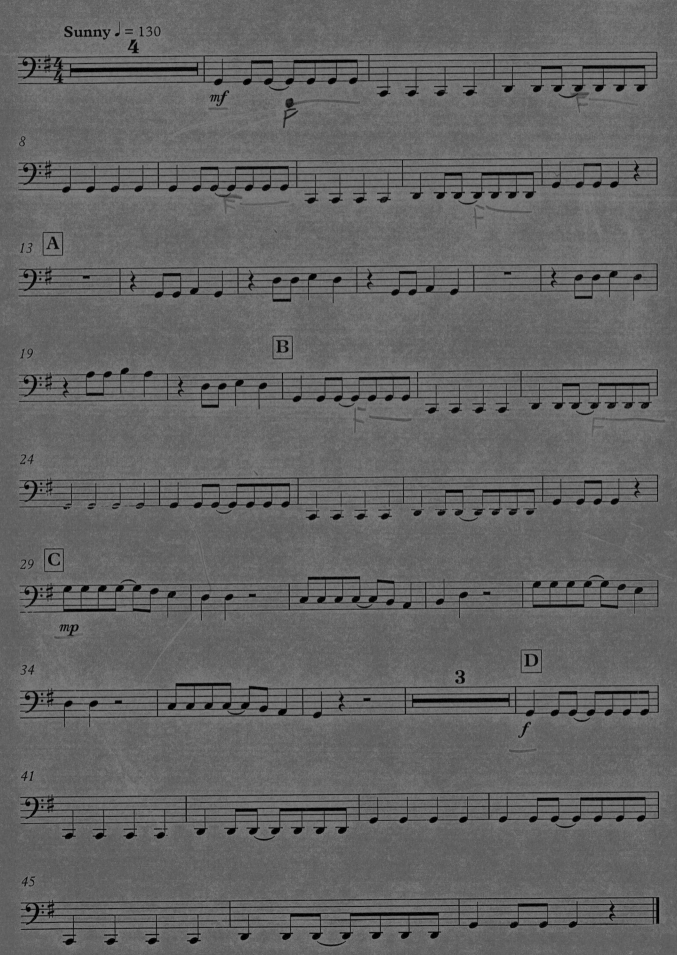

5 Go Tell Aunt Rhody

Folk Song

6 O Come, Little Children

Folk Song

7 May Song

Folk Song

8 Allegro

S. Suzuki

9 Perpetual Motion

S. Suzuki

Use repeat with first and second endings when accompanying Perpetual Motion and its variation.
When only Perpetual Motion (without variation) is played, use second ending and no repeat.

10 Long, Long Ago

T. H. Bayly

11 Allegretto

S. Suzuki

12 Andantino

S. Suzuki

13 Rigadoon

H. Purcell

14 Etude

S. Suzuki

B Variation in ♩♪♪♪

15 The Happy Farmer

R. Schumann

16 Minuet in C

J. S. Bach

17 Minuet No. 2

J. S. Bach

Suzuki® AND SUPPLEMENTAL PUBLICATIONS

NOTE READING

I Can Read Music for Cello
by Joanne Martin

Volume 1..00-0441

TECHNIQUE & PRACTICE

Double Stops for Cello
by Rick Mooney

Book 00-0761

Position Pieces for Cello
by Rick Mooney

Book 1 00-0762
Book 2 ....00-20572X

Thumb Position for Cello
by Rick Mooney

Book 1 00-0763
Book 2 00-0764

SOLOS & ENSEMBLES

Ensembles for Cello
by Rick Mooney

Volume 1.......................................00-0296S

I Know a Fox with Dirty Socks: 77 Very Easy, Very Little Songs for Beginners
by William Starr

Cello Book 00-25649

Magic Carpet for Cello – Concert Pieces for the Youngest Beginner
by Joanne Martin

Cello book with CD 00-27747
Piano Accompaniment 00-27014

Music Plus! An Incredible Collection
by William Starr

Cello Ensemble, or Cello with Violin
and/or Viola 00-14170X

Solos for Young Cellists
by Carey Cheney

Volume 1 Book 00-20810X
Volume 1 CD 00-21620X

TEXTBOOKS

Ability Development from Age Zero
*by Shinichi Suzuki,
translated by Mary Louise Nagata*

Book 00-0580

Diamond in the Sky (A Suzuki Biography)
by Jerlene Cannon

Book 00-40090

Nurtured by Love: The Classic Approach to Talent Education
*by Shinichi Suzuki,
translated by Waltraud Suzuki*

Book 00-0584
Spanish Edition 00-40330

Nurtured by Love, Revised Edition
*by Shinichi Suzuki,
translated from the Original Japanese Text
by Kyoko Selden with Lili Selden*

Book 00-39352

alfred.com

SUMMY-BIRCHARD INC.

ISBN-10: 0-87487-480-7
ISBN-13: 978-0-87487-480-8

9 780874 874808   50699